Learning Without Tears

LEARNING WITHOUT TEARS
(Children and Homework)

Dr. V. V. Bharathi
Reader, Dept. of Home Science
S.V. University, Tirupathi (A.P.)

Discovery Publishing House
New Delhi - 110002 (India)

First Published - 2001

Reprinted - 2017

ISBN: 978-81-7141-349-2

Learning without Tears

Published by:

DISCOVERY PUBLISHING HOUSE PVT. LTD.

4383/4B, Ansari Road, Darya Ganj

New Delhi-110 002 (India)

Phone: +91-11-23279245, 43596064-65

Fax: +91-11-23253475

E-mail: discoverypublishinghouse@gmail.com

sales@discoverypublishinggroup.com

web: www.discoverypublishinggroup.com

Printed at:

Infinity Imaging Systems

Delhi

Dedicated
To
PROF. S.R. VENKATRAMAIAH

Contents

Contents

Preface

Today's school-going child is the most stressed. Right from LKG level to IX Class children are stressed. Heavy load of syllabus, parental expectations, homework given by teachers, make the child helpless and unable to learn through play the basis of life. The child in his helplessness. is unable to cope with academic demands and fear of displeasing parents (because some schools threaten if the child fails to get 60 per cent and above he will be issued a transfer certificate), they are found to develop Bronchial asthama, ticles, stomach-aches, fevers tios and phobias. This book is written after interviewing many children, parents and teachers as part and parcel of research conducted in the department of home science. Some of the opinions of parents, teachers and children are given in appendixes.

Books of this type are expected to help parents and teachers in understanding the child's problems and to develop suitable means of helping children. After reading this book even if one parent/teacher tries to help his/her child/student to learn better, I deem that all the purpose of my writing this book is achieved. Let us all decide and determine to work to end this educational cruelty towards children and make learning a pleasurable exercise.

V. V. Bharathi

1

INTRODUCTION

Every parent is ambitious to see that his/her child comes out of his school in flying colours. In making their ambitions come true, sometimes children are send to school much before they are ready and the schools are selected not on the basis of the amenities it can provide and the qualifications of the teachers but on the number of subjects it can provide training and number of extra co-curricular activities. All this means today's child starts his process of learning with load of books on the back and tears in the eyes.

It is such a common sight in any town number of children well stitched in pinafares and the shoes however wrong fitting they are and stuffed into an auto or a cycle rickshaw to reach these so called convents or English Medium school.

English not being the mother tongue when offered as medium of instruction requires certain amount of drilling and perfection. Today it is a common topic (when a group of parents meet) that how much their children are learning or what home work is given; whether the child does it by himself or the parents help him. Sometimes there are certain schools which arrange for tuition classes soon after the school hours in order to complete the homework given during school hours. This makes a fun of the teacher and the idea behind giving homework.

Let us examine what is the meaning of this term *Homework.*

What is Homework ?

Any work that is done by child at home if helpful in reinforcing and supplementing, what has been studied at school, can be termed as 'homework'. It prepares the ground for further learning. It is most relevant activity among the after-school activities. Children devote much time everyday to do the homework. Teachers also devote a lot of time to assign and check homework.

According to Short Oxford English Dictionary prepared by William Little, H.W. Fouler and Jessie Coulson (1987) Homework means "lessons to be done by a school child at home".

The dictionary of education (1959) defines 'homework' as school assignments to be completed out of regular school hours at the residence of the pupil. The Websters third new international dictionary (1966) defines 'homework' as an assignment given to a student to be completed outside of the class room.

According to Chambers twentieth century dictionary 'homework' means work to be done at home especially for school.

Homework as Defined by Managerial Perspective

Homework as an important aspect of school program has been discussed by Ramaswamy (1992). According to Ramaswamy, managements by objectives - also known as MBO - is a powerful conceptual operational framework. An attempt has been made in his article to render framework management objectives to homework and recieved functions of management.

The three specific objectives of homework according to MBO principles are -

(a) Reinforcement-child needs reinforcement so that the learning experience is strengthened which inturn will facilitate retention.
(b) Remediation - Remediation involves identifying the areas of weakness in a particular child and assigning tasks to overcome the weakness thus noticed.
(c) Enrichment - Enrichment assignments are meant for brighter children, giving more challenging assigenements.

'Homework' makes a useful combination of children success at school. The child who returns after a few hours of learning in the school needs some follow up study at home which can be provided by the 'homework' assigned to him. Normally 'homework' is the repetitive form of work connected with the work done in the class room.

Assignment of homework is considered as one of the forms of adult centered or teacher centered methodology. The class room instruction is usually followed by home assignments, with the view that repetition of work creates a habit of doing a thing again and again, and helps children to retain the material learned by the student for a longer period. This device gives opportunity to children to plan and perform their work independently of the guidance and help of the teacher. It is a valuable means of study without the restriction of class work and supplements the teaching done in the class, improves the pupils ability and promotes better use of books and resources outside the school.

The main objectives of home work as summarised by Kochar (1985) are described below.

"Homework given in the class has the following objectives They are :

1. Stimulation of initiative, independence, responsibility and self direction.
2. Promotes development of permanent leisure time activities. interests in learning.
3. Facilitates enrichment of school learning experience, and
4. Reinforces the learning by further practice and application.

Homework establishes the habit of reading regularly, and sound study habits, a habit which goes a long way in the pursuit of knowledge. Again, it is with the help of those device parents are able to examine and inspect from time to time the work of their children and to suggest improvement with the cooperation of the teacher. Then home work if properly understood, skillfully planned intelligently assigned and sympathetically checked becomes indispensable and highly valuable.

According to Prahlad (1984) the following are the objectives of homework -

(a) to stimulate independent thinking, emotional stability and self direction,
(b) to develop permanent leisure time activities and interests in learning,
(c) to enrich school experiences and to make the pupils more responsible,
(d) to link previous and present learning,
(e) to reinforce the school learning by further practice and application,
(f) to encourage students to consult other bodies magazines, and journals apart from the prescribed text books,
(g) to help in individualizing instruction.

In order to achieve, the afore said objectives homework should be properly planned, made useful, interesting, creative and should suit the needs of both fast and slow learners. Probably the most valuable kind of homework involves children in activities which they can't have at school. It may be regarded as the continnum at one end at the other end as creative projects or experiments undertaken voluntarily by pupils.

However, the trends about giving home work or no home work have been following in quick succession. Let us examine the trends and practices regarding homework and school children especially during primary school period.

2

HISTORICAL TRENDS AND PRACTICES REGARDING HOMEWORK AND PRIMARY SCHOOL CHILDREN

Historically attitudes towards homework have been vacillating considerably. During 1910-1920 general attack on homework for eg: see the Ladies Home Journal Editorial (1913) on the 'Useless and really dangerous practice of carrying books home and asking pupils to do evening studies" seemed to have produced a decrease in the amount of required homework (Weiner 1912). Again during 1930 - 1940 opposition to homework seemed to have decreased the amount of homework (Gold Stein, 1960, Holtman, 1969). In the post sputrok period 1957-67, the new maths seemed to have been accompanied by demands for more homework. (Bond and Smith, 1966, Hedges, 1964) surveys during this period indicated rather wide acceptance of homework by parents, teachers and pupils (Bond and Smith, 1966); Check (1966), Kerzic (1966) NEA Survey (1970). It seemed likely that during 1968-1977, the pressure to give more homework has decreased. However Buffio and Shane (1977) reported that the these reports of National Education Association, asked to poll 1700 principals in what ways SSC schools have changed in the last five years, half the elementary schools, three fourths of the secondary schools reported an increase in homework. This is hardly surprising when one reflects on the growing instances that schools offer more demanding as well as more interesting instruction programmes.

The Problem

The editorial of the medicopsychological journal 'mind' (1989) mentioned the observation made by Prof. B. Battacharjee, (a clinical psychologist from Calcutta), in his study for three years. He noticed over a period of three years, the number of children studying in English medium schools belonging to the age group of 8-14 years, lost their mental balance for the conflict caused by inability to cope up with the syllabi prescribed by the authorities and expectation of the parents. The study observed apart from the common neurotic trends and phobia reactions, psychosomatic illness like bronchial asthama, breathing trouble with palpitation headache, pains allover the body stammering etc. were found in a number of school children, especially those who are studying between I and IV standards in English medium schools. The sole reason being fear of failure to satisfy the school authorities (their threat of driving the child away from school with a transfer certificate if he scores less) anxieties and tensions on the part of the parents, also, do contribute to the frustration and consequent break down. The editor of 'mind' says if younger generation 'the future of nation' is affected so much something necessarily need to be done. It is high time that we should think of a change, especially in the syllabi of primary school education system to suit the socio-economic environment and also the psychological aspects of growing children.

News items on local daily *Eanadu* dated 2.4.92 reporting the uning of the hand of a school girl for not doing homework by new teacher, in the same daily on 15.2.92 a small girl was made to run away from the house because her mother would beat her black and blue if she failed to do the homework. Prof. Shanmugam in his community psychology (1985) mentions the main reason for school dropouts is their inability to cope up with syllabi and failure to do the home assignments, as a result, fear of punishment from the teacher in the class room and parents at home for getting low marks.

The letters to the editor column of women are dated September 15, 1990 by one parent which mentions about a U.K.G. child was made to write 50 pages a day. 31 pages of homework and 21 pages of class work and an equal number of papers for reading. The parent wishes that some one approaches the president of India with a petition on behalf of these innocent children in order to save from such *educational cruelty*.

Hoppock (1977) from the New Jersey department of education commented that "so many children today suffer from emotional problems which have lead to peptic ulcers in small children. His concern was properly better understood by parents with intellectually immature but conscientious children who become depressed or misbehave because of their inability to cope with homework.

It is hardly surprising when one reflects on the graving insistence that schools offer more demanding as well as more interesting instructional programmes with stress on grades, these days rather on learning and child's own progress; parents often feel, that they must help their children to get good marks. Often this compels them either to do most of the assignments themselves to correct the child's work to such an extent that it becomes their product and not his.

Sharma (1983) explained that students attitude towards homework were made known by the NCERT study. A staggering 82.6% of children interviewed in Maharashtra felt that they had to curtail their play hours to do the homework (which stops their most enjoyable activity). The student knows that the sooner the homework is done the earlier he can return to more pleasurable persuits. British Children of the same study took serious attitude towards homework. 70 per cent o them do the homework with their T.V. on and 25 per cent have played the music when they completed homework. The author concludes that Indian Children are over loaded with homework, with a long duration of time taken for completing (being tiresome). It should not exceed the well accepted norm of 90 minutes. Otherwise lack of feed back and the danger of negative attitude dislodge the merits of homework.

Mittol (1991) of the academy of paediatrics has warned the schools that academic force feeding will produce only Zombies rather than creative individuals. This clearly tells and supports the dictum that monotonous homework kills the creativity of the child.

Need for Reconsideration

The problem has reacted such herculian dimension, it made the most celebrated writer like R.K. Narayan (1985) to lament how the school child's burdened with loads of homework and how the enjoyable process of learning things is becoming painful and the child is loosing his childhood young under the drudgery of schooling.

All most all the studies that were conducted on homework in primary school stage, parents' teachers and intellectuals stress, that, there is a great need for reconsideration. Palardy (1986) says that most schools do not have a homework policy. Many teachers give some homework to all children in the class. They do not grade the homework correctly and the author recommends the following suggestions for reconsideration. They are -

1. Ensure uniform understanding of homework policies among students and parents.
2. Do not assign any homework at primary grade level.
3. Individualize the homework to whatever extent possible.
4. Grade and return home assignments and
5. Coordinate the homework assignments with other teachers so that child will not be over burdened with a lot of homework from all the teachers.

Against the complaints and criticism that small children are burdened with heavy school bags, the Yashpal Committee(1989) was constituted to examine the homework policies and syllabi of various systems of schooling in India, in order to make the child go to school without tears and without learn school bag. However, one needs to consider the attitudes of the three parties concerned with a topic namely the teachers, parents and most important over being the child himself.

3

HOMEWORK FROM TEACHER'S POINT OF VIEW

What 'Homework' Means to the Teachers

Teachers cultivate the habit of reading and writing among pupils by giving homework. This habit reduces the tensions and additional burden experienced by the teachers while teaching in the class room so teachers favour homework.

Doing homework improve creative ability and sharpens the minds of pupils and develops deeper knowledge in the subjects. It also develops planning for future activities. All these reasons make teachers favour giving homework.

A cross cultural study by Chuansheng and Stevenson (1986) supports the above reasoning 260 teachers from Chicago, Taipi, Sengai Beiging were asked to describe possible positive effects of homework. The results reported are the following: American teachers most frequently mentioned two major positive effects reinforcing materials presented in classroom and developing personality such as improving children's self-image and independence. Teachers from other cities agreed with teachers of Chicago on the first point but not on the second point only 8 per cent of teachers from other cities have agreed where as 41 percent of teachers of Chicago mentioned the second point.

The negative effects of homework as such were denied by the 34 per cent teachers of Chicago, 28 per cent of teachers from Beiging,

40 per cent of Taipie and Sengai teachers. The major criticism about homework according to those teachers was that an overload of homework could cause a loss of interest in studying and that homework could lead to bad study habits.

Salend and Others (1989) revealed that teachers of elementary secondary schools meant for children with learning disabilities accepted giving homework. 85 per cent of the respondents had problems in getting the work completed. Suggestion for improving homework procedures are given including giving specific feed back on homework assignments, giving clear and explicit direction and involving parents in the homework process however.

In another study, Murphy and Decker (1989), collected information about homework from the schedules completed by 3,000 teachers from 92 high schools of Illinois. Beyond the issue of time, they examined the structure of homework, types of homework allotted to students, how it were reviewed and graded, the level of powerful support for homework as viewed by teachers being questionnaire method. Findings indicated that (a) reasons for non-completion of homework included forgetfulness (40%), not enough time (19%), failure to understand the assignment (6%), work or job (9%), too many assignments 6%, (b) Homework was granted by 88% of teachers while the remainder did not grade the work, (c) school and parental sources were not heavily employed to reinforce the importance of homework.

Padmaja (1991) explored the attitudes of teachers towards homework as part of study on homework and school children. All the teachers involved in her study agree upon the need for homework. However, they all emphasised that there should be some quality of homework according to the age and class.

Manjula (1993) interviewed 100 teachers 50 from Telugu medium schools and 50 from English medium schools of Tirupati (A.P.), using questionnaire approach, to measure the attitudes of teachers towards homework. She tried to find out what do the teachers mean by the term homework.

Table - 1

Showing the Frequency of Responses Given by Teachers

	Teachers Response	*Percentage of Teachers Appearing*
1.	Agree with Websters Dictionary Definition of Homework	18.00
2.	It is a Tool for Recapitulation	32.00
3.	Helps to Test Knowledge and Understanding	14.00
4.	Motivates and Develops Children's Creativity	36.00

A majority of (36%) teachers agree that homework is means of motivation and a tool to develop child's creativity. 32% of the teachers mean homework as a tool for recapitulation. Only 18% agree with the Webster's dictionary and 14% say that they mean homework is a tool to test the knowledge and understanding of children.

Socio-demographic factors like age, sex, social class type of family, birth order, educational qualifications did not have any significant influence on the attitudes of the teachers towards homework.

So it is only the management pressure as well as pressure from parents which influence the teachers attitudes towards homework. The mean scores of Telugu medium teachers (83) and English medium teachers (84) were examined. Teachers from Telugu medium schools communicate easily in the mother tongue and give such homework as reading and answering questions.

The case of English medium school teachers is different. They frequently face pressure from the management to satisfy those parents of the children who join their schools. If the parents are not satisfied with the performance of their children they may draw their children from those private English medium schools. So the managements always exercise pressure on teachers, to show improvement in children's performance and scores in tests. This may make these teachers from English medium schools to show more interest in giving lots of homework to children.

Table - 2
Teacher's Views About Recommendations Regarding the Forms of Homework Given by Teachers.

Forms of the Homework	*Always*	*Sometimes*	*Never*
Written form	97%	8.00	-
Questions and Answers	100%	-	-
Referring to books	-	24.00	76.00
Collection of Pictures	58%	32.00	-
Drawing pictures	42%	58.00	-
Preparation of models	8%	92.00	-
Preparation of riddles	-	19.00	81.00

Table - 3
Homework (repetitive form) Given by Teachers According to the Medium of Instruction

Head of Institution	*Once*	*Twice*	*Thrice*	*More than that*
Telugu	48.0	20.0	24.0	8.00
English	5.0	30.0	54.0	11.0

The data shows that a majority of teachers given always finding answers for questions as homework and in written form, while telugu medium teachers ask the children to do it once or twice (48%, 20%, 24% respectively). Majority of English medium teachers like to ask the children to write them once or two times (54% and 30%) respectively. However giving homework in written form is not advisable as children at the primary school level especially during Ist and 2nd standards; as children at these grade levels have nc control over their hand writing. If the written form of work is more, they feel it difficult and may not complete. Later this may result in loss of interest in doing homework.

Collection of pictures, drawings of pictures models and preparation of riddles, increase the creativity and exploratory skills among the children to improve the scientific attitude in children. The Academy of children's theatre (ACT) by Deepak Thimmayya of Bangalore successfully uses theatre as a mean to complete curricular effectively. According to Thimmayya 'when theatre is used to teach the subjects taught at school it can help build a child as no other art form does. It does not stop at being only a form of art. It is natural creativity and children have lots of it". There is a hundred per cent agreement among all the teachers. They agree that there should be some reconsideration about homework in primary classes because the homework at these levels must be age appropriate and suitable to the abilities of the children.

The following are the reasons given by teachers for considering age before giving any homework. They are :

1. Small children cannot concentrate for longer periods.
2. The much of homework fatigues and frustrate the children.
3. Children should not be subjected to mental and physical stress and strain due to excessive homework.

These responses regarding reconsideration coincide with the suggestions made by Prahlada (1984). They are :

- more school time should be devoted to the guidance of meaningful learning.
- Homework should be properly organized to provide novelty.
- Students should be encouraged to do more reading and studying of the kind that will have continuing value in later life,
- Students should be given more freedom and choice in the matter of,

what, how and when and with whom to study;

- Instead of writing homework in note books teachers can encourage children to write homework on loose sheets and these sheets can be preserved safely in a file.
- Homework should be more individualized, meaningful and useful.

Almost all the (100 mothers and 100 fathers) of 100 Telugu medium school children opined that homework need to be given daily where as 60% mothers and 50% of fathers of children from English medium school demanded homework on weekly basis. 40 per cent of parents of school children favoured homework thrice a week on subject rotation basis.

Table - 4

% Responses of Parents About the Need for Homework

S.No.	Need	Telugu Med.		English Med.	
		Mothers	Fathers	Mothers	Fathers
1.	To improving academic standards (a) Improve hand writing (b) to maintain continuity (c) Remind the lessons (d) to help the child to get good marks	97	100	95	95
2.	To make the child feel responsible and reduce wandering	90	80	55	60
3.	To improve memory and concentration	98	65	60	64

Majority of parents of children from Telugu medium schools emphasize the need for homework against its positive effects when compared with parents of children of English medium schools. The percentage of responses of English Medium parents get reduced to a little above half the percentage responses of parents of children studying in telugu medium schools. This is a clear indication that parents are aware of the monetary of homework give to their children.

4

HOMEWORK - PARENTS' POINT OF VIEW

Parents have a key role in children's academic programme. The attitudes of the child follow the parental model. Child's academic performance and interest in academic activities depend upon the values attached to education, learning process and the extent of involvement from the parents. In a study conducted by Padamja (1991) 200 mothers and 200 fathers of 20 primary children studying, (100 from telugu medium school and 200 from English medium schools) asked the parents what they mean by 'homework'. Almost all the parents of these children expressed that homework is "the work given to the child to be performed at home."

Only 5 per cent of the fathers of children from English medium schools expressed that homework is not necessary for children during primary school age as they think that children during this stage is too young to do tedious homework. They want to engage them in play, which is their right. If it is denied to children and if they are forced to do lot of homework they may lose interest in learning, develop negative attitude and refuse to attend the school. Rest of the parents of both the English medium and Telugu medium school children expressed favourable attitudes towards homework emphasizing the need for homework during primary school age.

In general parents have favourable attitudes and expectation towards homework of their children. Parents irrespective of their income group, education and employment status attach much importance to their children's education. It is a recent trend where parents realized the importance of education and show greater involvement in attending to their children's homework. In most cases it is the parents who go and ask the teachers, to give more homework to their child in order to keep him engaged; and 'avoid him from wasting time in useless persuits like play'. Some parents do the homework by themselves in the name of helping, where home work loses its significance and meaning. Some parents help their children totally and some may supervise the child doing his/her homework. A majority of parents of children from English medium schools send their children for extra tuition which may in turn prove cumbersome to the child.

What happens generally in many cases is parents do not know how to help their children with the homework. Sometimes the child correctly perceives that the parents have taken over the responsibility for his homework. He thinks that they are so anxious about the entire matter. What was typically found was that the child who finds, that his parents do not trust him to do well on his own, decides that he will let them take over completely. He stops doing the homework without parents' help.

Parental Involvement in Children's Homework

Just like any other activity of learning the presence of an elderly person provides a lot of emotional equity to the child. There is enough research evidence which demonstrates clearly the contributions of parental involvement in children's homework. A few research studies showing the importance of parental attitudes in children's homework are required Hoppock (1977) of Newjersy department education commented that many school children suffer from emotional problems; as result the American Medical Association felt compelled at its convention to have special symposia on peptic ulcers in children. Hoppocks' concern was only understood by parents with intellectually immature but conscientious children who become depressed or misbehave because of their inability to cope with the given homework. In a study conducted by Shivasankar Reddy (1984) the rural sample of parents had least favourable attitude towards their child's education.

Burks (1986) analysed the longitudinal data to study home learning program on reading achievement and found that higher level of reading achievement was seen in children who had parent child interaction , using school designed reading activities at home coupled with and correlated with teacher instruction at school. However Keiths (1986) examination of direct and indirect of T.V. Time, homework and parental involvement on high school seniors achievement having 28051 children indicated that homework had an important positive effect on student achievement and T.V. Time had a small negative effect and parental involvement had no direct affect on their achievement scores but did positive influence on their homework. Further analysis of the data has shown that possibilities of low homework demands and of excessive T.V. viewing for given the time spent on T.V. and homework and their influence on achievement.

There are some general statements used by parents, as part of their involvement, regarding the homework of children, as enlisted by Fisher and Fisher (1956).

(a) You cannot go out and play until you do your homework.
(b) Let me check your homework, before you put your notebook away
(c) How can you do your homework while you are watching T.V.?
(d) Get off the telephone and do the homework.
(e) I will give you more pocket money if you get to average in your homework.
(f) Your homework looks stoopy to me.
(g) I am going to talk to your teacher, about what we can get you to take homework more seriously.

Sometimes people are concerned about the occupation and educational level of parents. This leaves us with a question "Do educated parents, and parents with profession really help their children regarding their homework? The answer is somewhat unclear. It is observed by the author uneducated parents though are not in a condition to help the child regarding homework, arrange for tuition which in turn increases their homework load because they are made to do some extra homework at tuition. Sometimes it is also possible that uneducated parents take refuge in their helpless but demand the child some how learn and clear the homework.

In a cross cultural examination of one work Harold Setvenson found the amount of time spent by mothers per week (1989) and it reveals a significant trend. The estimates for how much time the mothers spent with child's home work was significantly higher for Chinese children than for American children. Mothers generally believed to help in reading than in Mathematics. However in all cultures the first graders were given more assistance than the 3rd and 5th grades.

Table - 5
Amount of Time Mothers Help with Homework
Number Minutes / Week

	American		*Chinese*		*Japanese*
	Chicago	*Minneapots*	*Beizing*	*Taipe*	*Soudai*
Study I					
Grade I	-	96	-	189	160
Grade 5	-	100	-	100	102
Study II					
Grade 5	-	138	-	142	187
Study III					
Grade 1	282	-	-	949	194
Grade 5	168	-	-	307	90
Grade 5					
Study IV					
Grade 1	221	-	420	-	-
Grade 2	204	-	282	-	-
Grade 3	194	-	264	-	-

The fathers in the studies 3 and 4 were asked how much they helped their children on mathematics. Estimates were lowest for American fathers than for Chinese fathers. In Chicago 24% of fathers said they help their children 15 minutes/day. In Beiging the percentage was 44%, Taipe 36% in seadai 32%.

In a study conducted in S.V. University (1991) the results revealed that 80% of mothers and 40% of fathers of the English medium schools help their children regarding homework when compared with 60% mothers and 30% fathers of Telugu medium school children involved in this particular study.

Table 6
Time and Frequency of Parental Assistance to Children in Doing Homework

Time and Frequency	*Telugu Medium*		*English medium*	
	Mothers	*Fathers*	*Mothers*	*Fathers*
1 hour/day	0	0	35	0
2 hours/day	-	-	-	-
According to available time	60	10	45	40

Majority of the mothers who spend 1 hour per day in assisting their children were having children studying in the lower classes (1 and 2 classes) and this is in conformity with results described by Stevenson's study. Father's participation of assistance is very much low and they assist whenever they find time. To help on a regular basis is almost an impossibility, because of their busy schedule and this sort of assisting children calls for a lot of patience which is present in abundance and personified only among the mothers.

The prevents differ in proportion of assistance given to children in doing their home work the data collected in this study by Padamja (1991) is subjected to t-test for proportion.

Mothers differed significantly from fathers in giving assistance to their children (Table 7). The possible reason for the difference may be that mothers maintain a close relationship during childhood years and mothers tend devote a lot of time on their children in order to fulfil their unfulfilled wishes.

Table 7
Proportion of Parental Assistance to Children in Doing Homework

Medium	*Mother*	*Father*	*t*	*P*
T.M.	0.60	0.30	4.264*	.5 level
E.M.	0.80	0.40	6.773*	.5 level
t	3.086* (*5 level)	1.482		

In yet another study (1992) mothers' involvement was found to be influenced by the medium in which the child studied. Out of 100 mothers (50 mothers of children from English school, and 50 mothers of children from Telugu medium school) 5 mothers of category I said they help the children against 10 mothers of second category. It was surprising fact that mothers who did not help were not illiterates. They were not able to help their children because they were busy with household work, taking care of younger siblings of this child and other activities.

Do Educated Parents Really Help ?

The education level of fathers and mothers also seem to affect the child's academic stress. F 83.857 significant at .01 level and mothers education level also seem to affect the child academic level. F = 77.704 (Krishna Kumari 1994). This is explained in terms of 'the parents being the first teachers, the dependency is at a high level. Educated mothers gave more help as they were closer to their children upto second grade level.

However Lalitha Subrahmanyam (1992) stated "majority of the parents of present generation, having had their education in the regional language as the medium of instruction, are not in a position to coach their children in English.

But having highly educated parents has its repercussions too: Because majority of teachers in private schools leave it to the responsibility of parents to give good coaching, parents are forced to take up the responsibility. If parents fail to take care of the academic needs/demands of their children, it will lead to tension among children. This is more so when both parents are busy with their job work. Lack of time leads to tension, impatience and resentment in -parents towards the needs of the children. Besides job, parents can't become teachers on fulltime basis (Lalitha Subrahanmanyam, *The Hindu* 31st March 1992).

However the results obtained by Desphande and Saraswathi, (1987) from studying 224 parents shown that parents did not differ in their attitudes towards homework given to their children. Leach et al (1990) investigated on the parental involvement in teaching of reading, taking parents of 40 children in two Ist grade class rooms and the results strongly suggested increase in reading rates when parental involvement was greater. Thus it may exact a lot of influence on the children's attitudes towards homework especially when the parents provide accurate and constructive feedback and interact in reinforcing manner.

5

CHILDREN AND HOMEWORK

The party directly concerned here is the child. Bhattacharjee's (1985) observation in his clinic is really an eye opener. One of the reasons observed by Prof. Shunmugam (1985) for large number of school dropouts is their inability to understand and cope with the demands/ pressure caused by school work (which is large constituted by home work). The socio-demographic variables which affect other aspects of his behavior also affect this aspect of home work.

Children's Attitude Towards Homework

Children during early elementary school years have a tendency to play. They learn the rules and code of conduct that prepares their future life, only by following rules and regulations dictated by their peer group (a mini society) during active play. This golden opportunity they are denied due to increased academic pressure by means of lots of home work and a myriad of subjects to be covered.

74% of children studied by Padmaja (1991) revealed that they dislike homework. The reasons being the heavy load of homework and severe punishment for not coping up with the homework demands from teachers as well as parents. The important reason given by majority of children is non-familiarity of the child with the language in which home work is given and sufficient or lack of help from their parents. Sometimes parents even threaten their children that they will be punished if they won't finish the homework (News item in *Andhra Jyothi*, 1992).

Some children said that they don't like homework as it leaves no time to play, mothers won't allow to play, unless home work is completed. By the time the work is done it will be dark, no one will be there to play with. This makes the child to suppress his desire, and anger about his inability to play reflected in the drawings of many school children -- mothers represented as cruel ring masters, teachers pictured to be having long teeth and demonish features, picture of child is drawn as if he / she is a cage. This sort of tends will affect the psyche of the children and may result in 'burnt out syndromise'.

Just like any other aspect of child's behavior, homework attitudes are also affected by socio demographic factors. These will be discussed in detail in the following paragraphs. Age of the child is an important factor which influence his motor skills, eye-hand coordinators and language skills that are necessary to meet the requirements of first standards. The importance of the principle of readiness cannot be over - emphasized. The child to be joined in first class must have accomplished language skills, eyehand coordination; motor skills necessary to hold the pencil/pen and to sit for at least half an hour to one hour at a stretch. Age and grade were viewed as synonymous in this context.

The results of the series of studies conducted on the human development section of home science department, S.V. University are real eye openers for teachers, parents and other policy makers. In all these studies children from lower classes (I, II & III class) belonging to 5[+], 6[+], 7[+] years dislike home work, children from IV and V classes vary in their responses as a majority of the confessed having do homework as they have no other way to escape punishment from the parents.

Table 8
Children's Attitudes Towards Homework

	I		II		III		IV		V	
(n=20)	E.M.	T.M.	E.M.	T.M.	E.M.	T.M.	E.M.	T.M.	E.M.	T.M.
Dislike homework	20	17	13	10	2	0	0	0	0	0
Do not like home work	0	3	7	10	18	20	20	17	20	20

Table 9
ANOVA Effect of Age, Sex and Medium on Children's Attitude Towards Homework (1991)

Source of Variation	*D.f.*	*S.S.*	*MSS*	*F - Value Calculated*	*p*	*Critical*
Age	4.	10.40	2.60	1.7568	NS	2.40
Sex	1	0.36	0.36	0.2438	NS	3.96
Medium	1	6.76	6.76	0.5676	NS	3.96
Age x Sex	4	7.04	1.76	1.1892	NS	2.48
Sex x Medium	4	0.36	0.36	0.2438	NS	3.96
Age x Sex medium	4	6.64	1.66	1.1216	NS	2.48
Error	80	118.40	1.40	--	NS	2.48
Total	99	157.00	---	---	---	---

This necessitates a slower weaning from preprimary class to regular classes. Everyday sometimes needs to be devoted by school authorities for involving the children in free play, creative activities and rhymes which may be decreased gradually as the grade increases.

Sex of the Child

Sex of the child has a definite impact on how the child is treated and affected in his environment. Many parents and other relatives sniff off when the new born child is a girl. Whereas a boy is a wellcome guest.

The results of the two studies conducted in 1991 and 1992 show that the boys and girls did not differ in their attitude towards homework (Table 9).

However Deshpande and Saraswathi (1989) demonstrated that secondary school girls differ significantly from boys of the same age group in their favourable attitudes towards homework. Girls had a significantly more positve attitudes.

Medium of Instruction

English is not being the mother tongue, one may need to study and put a lot of efforts if children are to achieve maximum score parents would like to have their children to join English medium schools. The load of subjects is great as observed by Venkata Subbaiah (*The Hindu*, May 24, 1994) the survey on school bag revealed "that the weight of school bag in private sector English medium public school is more than 4 Kgs while it is around 1 Kg in rural primary schools. The school bag of a primary school child in a Panchayati Raj and Municipal School carries a slate and four small text books and four note books. But in the case of English medium schools the child is expected to carry for instance in II grade age group 6+ years, text books of English, mother tongue, Hindi, Maths, Science, Social Studies, moral science, besides three to four note books for each subjects. One for class work and one for homework. Besides this he requires to take other work books, pocket book, diary and so on. This leaves the child no time or chance for physical exercise.

In a recent research Venkatalakshmi and Bharathi (1995) reported that English medium School children reported more anxiety than their counterparts from Telugu medium schools. Padmasri (1992) reported that academic stress adversely affected the health status of the individual and family support is beneficial to academic achievement. Krishna Kumari (1994) reported that children from English medium differ significantly in experiencing academic stress from Telugu medium school children as shown in following Table.

Table 10
Medium as a Source of Stress in Children

Medium	*No.*	*Mean*	*S.D.*	*T-value*	*p*
English	75	9.88	5.85	12.671**	.01 level
Telugu	75	20.48	4.27		

The explanation offered is that in Telugu medium schools the teacher pupil ratio is high. Single teacher takes classes at a time for 2 or 3 different classes resulting in little or no attention for children. In case of English medium school children the load is more and too vigilant a teacher, over demanding parents, punishment from school authorities with a transfer certificate in case the child failed to meet the standards set by the school authorities making them more prone to experience academic stress.

Type of Family

The child's first education starts in the family. The language, reading and writing skills and other necessary associated social skills are learnt only in the family. Family also act as a reinforcement agent when parents help the child, in understanding the academic persuits, in proper perspective.

Just like any other familial variable, type of family may exert its influence on the child's attitudes towards homework and stress. Krishna Kumari (1994) studied the effect of family type and academic stress experienced by children and reported that children from joint families scored less stress scores than children from nuclear families on unequal subsamples. Though the difference was not statistically significant.

Table 11
Family Type and Stress Experienced by Children

Family	*n*	*Mean*	*Sol.*	*t-value*	*P*
Joint family	25	14.64	7.39	0.400	N.S.
Neuclear family	125	15.29	7.36		

Further probe into this dimension using equal sample may through some light on the effect of neuclear family in causing more stress in children.

Family size also sometimes influence the interaction of the child.

Families with one or two children have less anxiety and stress (Bharathi and Venkatramaiah, 1976). The results reported by Krishna Kumari (1994) show that family size significantly influences the stress scores of children. Children from small families (i.e. with one or two children) experienced less scores than children from large families with three or more children.

Table 12

Family Size and its Effect on Stress Score

Number of Children	*n*	*Mean*	*Sd.*	*t*	*P*
Upto 2 children	75	12.36	7.03	5.071**	.01 level
3 and more children	75	18.00	6.59		

Smaller the family size greater will be the interactions and parents are bound to pay more attention and more demanding.

Birth order is another variable which often affect the individual's behavior. The first born child experiences more anxiety than later born with certain exceptions (Bharathi and Venkatramaiah, 1976). In families with larger number of children who have grown up before another is born. The last child himself is paradoxically in the position of first child. The last child gets best attention sometimes (Adler, 1952).

Table 13

Analysis of Variance Between Birth Order and Stress of the Child.

Source	*Df*	*S.S.*	*M.S.*	*F*
Between group	2	483.26	241.63	4.633**
Error	147	7666.88	552.16	
Total	149	8150.41		

The mean scores obtained by first born in 14.76, second born = 13.96 and later borns 18.33 :

Intelligence and children's attitude towards home work,

Intelligence is an independent variable. Many factors may influence the intelligence of children like genetics, home and environment and interest of the children. Many studies co related attitudes towards home work with intelligence (Keith, 1992, Krishna 1983, Paschal 1984; Sasikala and Deshpande, 1984). Some have shown the relationship between the variables as positive and some others have demonstrated negative relationship. Sudharani (1993) correlated the intelligence scores on Raven's progressive matrices and scores on attitude form of home work and found that there was a close significant positive relationship between intelligence scores and children's home work attitudes (r = 0.212) when the subsamples pertaining to lower grades the scores correlated re-negatively with intelligence scores (Table - 14)

Table 14
Correlation Coefficient Between Attitudes Scores and Intelligence Scores of Children

Group	*Total sample*	*I Class*	*III Class*	*V Class*	*VII Class*	*IX Class*
n	100	20	20	20	20	20
r	0.212	-0.15	-0.18	0.30	0.58	0.52

A close observation of these results revealed that children studying in I to III classes, those having high intellectual scores did not have positive attitudes toward homework. However from V class onwards there the trend reverses and high positive correlation is seen between intelligence and attitudes toward homework. Theoretically speaking children with high intellectual abilities have deep involvement in all academic procedures and persuits. This is possible only when the home work is given to them is challenging and interesting. The lowerclass children (I to III classes) though intelligent, their scores did not correlate positively with home work attitudes as the work given at this stage is mere repetition of writing the words or answers 5 times or 10 times. This will be very mechanical and not challenging to the child. This is further supported by the results reported by Sasikala and Despande (1984) using under achievers (those who occupy top score position on intelligent test scores and get less marks in a class test deviced by the teachers). The experimental group scored better on post test when the means were adjusted and previous achievement. This may be attributed to the need based home work. Tom and Eric (1992) studied the effect of home environment and maternal intelligence as predictors of verbal intelligence in a comparative study of pre-schoolers with elementary school children and reported a significant relation between home environment and verbal intelligence when the affect of maternal intelligence was a significant predictor. It is obvious that intelligent mothers stimulate their children better and provide concrete, direct first hand experience to their children. The quality of assistance, methods adopted may stimulate the factor of intelligence present in the child and may create a stimulating, conducive environment when the mother has superior intelligence.

6

NEED FOR RECONSIDERATION

The observation made by Prof. Bhattacharjee (1989), Clinical Psychologist were quoted in the editorial of '*Mind*' which illustrates the gravity of situation "Apart from common neurotic trends and phobie reactions psychosomatic illnesses like bronchial asthma, breathing, trouble with palpitation, headache, pain all over the body, stammering etc. are found in a number of cases especially, those children studying between Ist and 4th Standards. From 1989-91 he observed a number of school children especially from English medium schools consisting of 8-14 years of age; lost their mental balance because of the conflict caused by the failure to cope with the syllabi prescribed by the school authorities, and the expectations of the parents. Sharma (1983) in his article about homework in India and abroad quotes a staggering 82.6% per cent of children from Maharashtra (who were interviewed in a study) felt they had to curtail their play hours so as to complete homework and they know that the earlier the work is done they can turn to more pleasant persuits. However a British study quoted by Sharma has indicated its sample took a very serious attitude towards homework. 70 per cent of the sample completed homework with their T.V. on end about 25 per cent of the sample always played music while completing homework. Thus however tells that Indian children loathe homework, as they are over burdened with it. Mittol (1991) from the academy of paediatrics has warned the parents that academic force-feeding will produce academic Zombies , rather than individuals with originality and creativity. Famous novelist R.K. Narayan once aptly said in Rajyasabha about the heavy load of school bag and stressed upon the need to reduce the school bag load as it has become synonymous to child labour. Childhood should have chance to bloom, rather than within the process of learning. It was also termed as 'educational cruelty' towards young children, as children are not allowed to enjoy their childhood in play and other persuits which improve the quality of their life. A parent in letter to the editor of *Femina,* even has gone to the extent of asking the press to request the President of India to end this educational cruelty towards young children.

This sort of over taxing may result in burning down syndrome where children get exhausted even before they are introduced to the intricacies of learning because of parental force feeding (Mittol 1991). This sort of fear has led a few parents to deschool and help small groups of four to six children by like minded parents. Though it has its own advantages like a tensions free atmosphere, and convenience to learn at one's own speed under parental care. However it has the disadvantage of lack of opportunities for socializing.

It is undebatable fact some sort of reinforcement in the form of homework is necessary. How much is too much? What about the quality and the standards? are the factors that boggle the minds of parents' teachers and human developments students.

A series of research work conducted in S.V. University from the year 1991 to 1995 by Padmaja (1991), Suneetha (1992), Sudharan: (1993), Manjula (1994), Krishna Kumari (1994), Sribhrgavi (1995) stress about the need for reconsideration about the homework. Parents, teachers and young children agreed that there is a need for reconsideration.

Human Resource Development (HRD) Ministry of Government of India has appointed Yashpal Committee (1992) to reduce the school bag load.

The Yashpal Committee

This committee was appointed by the Human Resource Ministry with Prof. Yashpal, former Chairperson of U.G.C. as Chair person along with eight panel members to survey the wide spread criticism of huge size school bag which lay parents and teachers felt was turning learning as drudgery. Appointment of this committee was done by Mr. Arjun Singh, the then Human Resource Development minister, based on the report of national advisory committee on reducing study load on children in 1992. "The weight of school bag represents one dimension of the problem, another could be in child's daily routine. Right from early childhood, many children, especially those belonging to middle classes are made to slog through homework, tuitions and coaching classes of different kinds. Leisure has become a scarce commodity in the child's especially the urban child's life". (National Advisory Board on Education Report, 1992). The committee was asked to advise how to reduce the load of children at all levels while improving the quality of learning.

The experts of Yashpal Committee as well as the journalists feel that the loaded school bag could well be on its way out and Jack could be saved from ending up as a dull boy, if the recommendation of national advisory committee on reducing book load on children is accepted by the government. The committee in its report (March, 1993) has suggested the abolition of the school bag and homework at preschool levels. It also suggested a ban on tests and interviews for admissions to nursery classes. The committee headed by Prof. Yashpal favoured legislative and administrative measures, ensure an overdose of learning is not inflicted on children especially during the former five years.

Calling for a radical change in the nature and character of home work the report suggests that in the primary classes children should not be given any homework save for extension of explorations in home environment. Even at the upper primary and secondary school level, the homework need be compulsory and where necessary it should be non-textual.

The committee also criticized the 'catching up syndrome' which has led 'the parents and teachers to expect their children to perform thus killing 'the joy of learning. Competitions where individual achievement is rewarded 'need to be discouraged since they deprive children of joyful learning. It says pointing out, that the problem, is conceptual and can not be fully addressed through easily manageable administrative actions'. It needs discussion and academics, thinkers need to think over this basic problem ".

Suggestions Based on Observation of Common Types of Homework Given in School

As part of practical importance, the homework activities given in ten private English medium schools were observed for one week and these observations revealed interesting general trends for all three classes.

Table 15
Types of Homework Given in Local Schools

Type	*Quantity*	*Frequency of Responses*
Writing of words repeatedly	3 pages every day in all subjects	6
Writing questions and answers	5 times each question 6 question/subject	10
Filling the blanks	10 sentences 10 times/sentence	5
Matching	Words from A & B columns	3
Drawing of pictures	Only once	3
Mathematics	Sums were also asked to be done 10 times/	10

This has lead the children to take homework as a cumbersome one especially during Ist standard. The intensity and severity increased when monthly test and mid-term examinations are fast approaching. This overloading/pressurising is making the children to develop negative approach not only towards homework but towards the entire process of learning.

The author of this book feels that there should be no homework for children upto 5 classes. Even if there is it must be oral work along with explorations in home environment. Class room experience need to be presented in an interesting manner. The child needs to be encouraged to learn using all the five senses through self discovery. For this providing a lot of direct purposeful first hand experience is very necessary.

Suggestions Given by Experts

Famous Kannada author Dr. Sivaram Karanth says - "If you leave children to their own creativity, they can be inspired and original. In the words of his eldest daughter Dr. Malavika Kapur, Clinical Psychologist at National Institute of mental health and neuroscience Bangalore " my father thought that it was not necessary for young children to sit in a class room for eight hours as any school was bound to make us to do. Dr. Karanth had been experimenting with children's education over since 1920 and he recalls when he asked village children to get as many neutral colour pigments as they could find to an art camp one child brought thirty one different pigments for more than what children would have a class in a sophisticated art class. So he preaches and followed the method training children at home upto the age of nine or ten and later when they are ready can join formal schools, however he insisted that proper teaching methods are to be followed. In a documentary 'pressure taken' by the NCERT Dr. Shivaram Karanth says that it is time, we stopped boring and terrifying children alternately and insisted help them evolve into happy and creative adults.

Malavika Kapur in her book *Mental Health of Indian Children* (1994) writes "the family and the school are the strongest institutions in a child's life. The school can either act as a safety net protecting children from hazards that affect their development and well being, or as an agent that actually causes mental problems. According to her schools - particularly those catering to the urban middle class have stopped being fun many years ago. This is compounded by the parental anxiety that the child grows up to be a doctor or engineer. The out come of six hours of schooling and up to six hours more of homework, and tuition is that , the child is left with no time for play, peer interaction and/or hobbies. Parents have to choose whether they want their child to be original, creative and happy or just an educated Zomby.

Former Rajya Sabha member and English novelist R.K. Narayan has aptly said about joyless childhood and insisted that childhood should have a chance to bloom rather than wilt in the process of learning. One of the letters to the editor of *Women's Era* from a father of a 5½ year old child says that his child was asked to write a set of 120 dictation words 5 times which alone run to 30 pages in a note book and wished that children should be saved from educational cruelty.

Amuktha Mahapathra, principal of ABACUS Montessorie School says that our children are pressured too much. In the case of 6-12 years old age group mechanical pressure is there to perform, write and learn by role but there is no challenge to their imagination. Their intelligence is not addressed. Education seems to be more information based rather than knowledge based which necessitates enquiry, and is more scientific. These remarks convey that education should be knowledge based making the child to enquire and reason out in a scientific manner.

Sinha (1989) recommends that homework should not be given to children up to 10 years. A fair amount of oral work may be given by way of home assignment for older age groups homework should be consistent with sound educational principles and involve some thinking and application on the part of children. It should be varied, so as to include project work and collection of information materials. Whatever may be the homework it should be free from monotomy.

Lalitha Subrahmanyam suggests that it will be a welcome change for the child, to come home and move with other children in the neighborhood, play with them under the care and freedom given by their parents. This sense of freedom enjoyed by the child is different from that enjoyed at school. This is a restricted /discipline free, feel as you please, do as you like atmosphere. Moreover children of the age need to go out with their parents of enjoy a walk and talk to them. Such interactions strengthen the bond, love of affection between the child and parents. The tedious homework and assignments make them dull and leave no time to enjoy a happy home environment.

Leaving them in a 'friendly, neighbourly, homely and protected atmosphere' is in itself a 'learning process' and does a lot to promote their mental health and happiness.

Suggestions Given by Parents

According to the results obtained by Padmaja (1991) 300 parents of the school going children studying 1 to V classes in the local Telugu and English medium schools, the following suggestions were given by them :

1. Homework should be given according to the age of the child.

2. Teacher should encourage children to do the homework in an affectionate manner.

3. Parents of children from English medium school wished, that the teacher should supervise the child's attempt to do, the homework in and out of school tuition class as carried out by many private English medium schools.

4. Some parents suggested, that there should be a time table for home work in such a way that subjects can be allotted on rotation basis so as to reduce the heavy load of homework in all subjects on one day.

5. Some parents preferred allowing the child to consult dictionaries, extra references, collect pictures and prepare riddle related to subject matters.

Suggestions Given by Teachers

Other than the child important concerned with homework is the teacher . The teacher sample interviewed by Padmaja (1991) suggested that homework should be interesting in the children.

- Child should be encouraged to understand and do the homework.
- Completed homework must be corrected accompanied with law and or praise.

In yet another research by Manjula (1993) a majority of teachers suggested that age of the child should be given due consideration.

- Reading and writing key words as best method of homework for primary classes.
- Only one teacher suggested that questions which make the child reason out and apply the child room learning experiences should be

given as homework.

- Yet another teacher suggested preparation of models and collecting relevant materials as best form of homework.

Suggestions Given by Children

Children who are the real ones involved in the process of learning by doing homework should be considered before really revising the homework forms. A study by Sudha Rani (1993) reveals that children suggested the following forms of homework as mostly accepted for them.

- Drawing Pictures (93%)
- Making Models (92%)
- Finding Answers (72%)
- Collecting Objects and Relevant Materials (69%)

However 82 percent of children wished that their knowledge could be improved by participating in quiz and preparation for quiz in a mostly accepted form of homework for them.

7

RECOMMENDATIONS

The following recommendations are made by the author of this book based on the review of available research evidence.

1. There should be no homework given to children studying 1 to 5 classes.

2. Any reinforcement for learning experience may be provided by giving oral work.

3. Writing exercises should be restricted to a minimum.

4. Drawings, preparing models, collecting pictures should be included in homework.

5. Application of reasoning, opportunities to explore the home environment and neighbourhood should be provided while giving assignment.

6. If at all written homework is given it should be only in the form of objective type of questions which will not be burdensome for the child.

7. Irrespective of medium of instruction children need to be given minimum amount of homework so that the joy of childhood is not robbed from children.

APPENDIXES

Parents' Opinion

1

Mrs. Rajamma (30) is the mother of Gopi studying in the local English medium school. The child Gopi is just five years old completed his pre-school classes and joined class 1. He has all the necessary motor skills like scribbling, colouring, identification of shops, naming and is able to understand the meanings of the words.

Krishnamoorthy (45) the father of Gopi, is working as a clerk in the mandal office. He studied upto SSLC in those days under economic compulsions. He married Rajamma who is only literate and did not attend any school. Now education is given top priority in their family according to Mr. Krishnamoorthy. They want their child to stand first in the class and secure at least 80 percent marks.

"You have to encourage the child and see that he is engaged upto maximum time in studies. If the teachers give maximum homework that engages the child the whole day." A busy child is a healthy child and clever child according to Mrs. Rajamma that is why she says that she chose such a school where the child energies are to be utilised at the maximum, it does not matter even if they change a bit exorbitantly." Is it not a prestigious point for us to say that our child is studying in a private convent where Doctors, Professors and Engineers send their children for study."

"Since myself and my husband are not very highly educated, we want our two boys to study well and get a respectable place for the parents and the family in the society."

2

Mrs. Kishori is a Lecturer in Chemistry in one of the local government Colleges. Her husband is a Doctor. As a small girl, she wanted to become a doctor but she could not achieve it due to several family constraints. She wanted to fulfil her wish by making any one of her children a doctor.

"In the present day competitive world one needs to work constantly, that is why I insist Ramesh and Mukhesh to come first and always at the top rank. This needs a lot of practice. So I ask the teachers of my sons to give them more homework. Just before examinations I send them for extra coaching, but in other days I myself test and try to clarify their doubts which they express."

"Being educated parents we should help our children, see that they participate in all academic activities. Childhood is the best period where they can concentrate to the maximum. Since English is not our mother-Tongue, a child needs to develop mastery over English. This cannot take place overnight. That is why I insist that children should be always kept busy with reading or writing work."

3

Neelamma (35) and Raghavaiah (42) are the parents of Vimala. child from a local convent school. Raghavaiah is physically handicapped and runs a vegetable shop in the nearby colony. Neelamma helps her husband by bringing vegetables and other articles of interest for local consumers. Their daughter Vimala was admitted in Milton academy.

When questioned about her child's performance Neelamma says, "I will rip her skin out, if she does not study properly. I have spent my whole life earnings to admit her into the prestigious institution. I send her to school by 7.30 in the morning, take her lunch at 1 p.m. again at 4.30 give her something to eat, so that she can return home after attending to her tuition. I do not want her to spend her time like me in physical drudgery. If she does the homework given by teachers and gets good marks, I am even prepared to send her in medicine."

"Both myself and my husband are illiterates. So I want at least my daughters to learn to read and write so that she can become "something", earn a respectable place for the family in our society."

4

Professor Rekha is a mother of 15 year old Ravi an 10 year old Rani. Both the children are studying in a local English medium school. Literally she is afraid of the academic load children are expected to cover. Their father being on a transferable job comes only for weekends or holidays. Though both the parents are post-graduates and have all the necessary skills, they are not in position to spend long hours in helping their children's home-work.

Prof. Rekha says that she has to maintain a dependent, struggle hard to win the co-operation of all the members and aim high so that she can etch a place of her own in the academic galaxy. So she has no time. Ramana her husband who is a Bank officer says that he does not want to bother himself even on weekends when he wants to spend his time peacefully by relaxing.

When children's rank cards are given, everytime it ends up in a series of angerments trying to throw the blame on the opposite person for shrinking the responsibility of guiding the children. The final decision is sending them for private tuition which again results in extra homework in addition to school homework for children. They do school home-work and tuition, tuition homework in school.

5

Sridevi is an Office Clerk. She has a son studying in the local English medium school. For a weekend the child of seven years was asked to write from one to ten thousands both in figures and words four times, given two pages English work to be written for five times. Three maps for marking the geographical details of continents, four poems from second language to be learnt by heart.

According to Sridevi, educated parents somehow can cope up and help their children, if they decide to help but "what about those parents who cannot express themselves in English" If a small child is made to hold the pen in hand for such long time, the fingers will be swollen and the child is not able to complete the homework. My son literally cried saying that he is unable to hold the pen. Children by nature would like to play relax whenever they find time. It is more so on a Sunday. These teachers space the homework by having the time-table or rotation of subjects. She even feels that it is necessary that someone should represent about their educational cruelty towards the child to the President of India under violation of human rights.

Children's Views

1

Ramu (8) is studying in a local English medium school, when he was approached by the Investigator to say a few words about homework, he replied like this : "I do not like really the whole process of studies what is there. You are lord sometime. You have to learn it by-heart, read and write five times or ten times. Next day - a row get is taught. Though I don't like homework really, I cannot say that she will punish me and report my mother. My mother in turn will become a 'Bakshasi' (demon) and frightens me saying what happens of I won't study, who all will die if I fail how the family's social status and her prestige will be reduced."

"I wish to play foot-ball draw and point whenever there is some-time. But where is the time? I am asked to get up by 4.30 a.m. Attend to native calls and get ready; after a glass of milk I need to go to my class teacher's house, study till 8.00 a.m. and went home get ready to go to school. I return by 4.30 p.m. and have my snacks and next moment I have to be at my science teachers house to attend to tuition till 8.30 p.m. By the time I come home mamma and pappa will be waiting for supper and then I go to sleep. Where is the time for play"?

2

Lalitha (9) is a student of class three from a local English medium school. "Our school is peculiar. They say games in time table" but there is no playground for our school, in the beginning we were taught some number games but now even during that period our class teachers wants us to sit quietly and complete our 'homework' how can we do the homework at school? There is a period after 4.30 where we are all expected to do the homework under our teacher's supervision".

"After this when I come home it will be 5.30 and my mother insists that I should sit and read each day's lessons on that particular day otherwise she says that I may forget." When I grow up I will see that all schools will not have any homework at all and children will be given full freedom to play. I will start such a school where children enjoy by playing games of their liking."

3

Swati (8) studies in a local English medium school. She is good at studies. According to the teachers the girl never fails to attend the school and work given by teachers. Ever since she was prompted to class three she has been saying day dreaming and every now and then does not attend school.

This particular school has a faculty ward system. The teacher in-charge visited Swati's house and was taken aback when Swati's mother reported that Swati is not studying at all and cries everyday before starting to school.

The Kacher Mekhala asked Swati as to what the reason was? In her own words, Swati is "fed up with studies and getting bored to sit in one place hours together and repeat what teacher says. We are not allowed to go out and play in the playground though the school has a big playground with huge mango trees and neem trees. It will be beautiful to sit under the shade of the trees and play freely with mud and water. We are not allowed to play at home because mother want us to study, write the home work and we are not even allowed to play at school because there is motive. Even if we play during lunchtime our teachers ask us not to make noise and tell us to sit and read quietly or attend to pending homework."

4

Bhaswath is in second class. He started complaining about body pains and stomach ache continuously. Prior to this, he never complained like this. The family doctor examined and said there is no pathological evidence for this and told the mother to give him good food and allow the child to play freely.

After a month Uma Bhaswath's mother found that her son's health has improved but he cries to go to school everyday. The teachers complain that he is not doing the homework regularly. When she insists him to study well and sit tight on homework he develops the body pains and stomach-ache.

Casual observation revealed that it is a practice that homework is given in all the six subjects and everyday there will not be less than twelve pages, each page to be written five times and a lot of reading work. Literally Bhaswath is left with little for any other activity. Reema also complains that much of her spare time she has to spend in making the boy attend to the homework. If she has any socializing in the evening Bhaswath will not get any help from the mother.

Teachers' Views

1

Ramesh (30) is a teacher in one of the convent school. His M.A. Degree and B.Ed degree tells him that he has to be considerate and keep the age of the child in mind while giving homework. Children also like Ramesh Sir very much as he plays and tells children everything in the form of stories. When questioned about his opinions regarding current trends in giving homework especially in English medium schools he come out with interesting information.

"One-day our principal has called me to his room and introduced some parents. I could recognise the parents of Girish and Chitarya who are very bright in the class and answer very smoothly. When asked the reason the parents said that they have a complaint that their children are not given enough homework. They always play, saying 'Sir, has not given any homework'. "We want you to give our children sufficient homework so that they will not waste their time in play."

Ramesh feels sorry for the children at the same time he has to think about his job and his school and says that he is helpless when parents demand is for more homework.

2

Krishnaveni (30) works in local municipal elementry school. Her problem is "parents complain that the teachers from municipal schools are not teaching properly and do not pay any attention to children. Actually each teacher is to take care of a class of 60 to 65 children. Even if you give homework, to supervise and initialy, each child being given one minute. It will be one hour fifteen minutes for checking homework in one subject and the syllabus is too heavy. In between our responsibilities and deputation on other jobs like census work, election duty and so on. Whatever little work we give children do it.

"Sometime ago I worked in a rural school when children attended school only when they did not have any festival to celebrate or farm work to be done. How are we as teachers to improve quality of education."

3

Kesari Babu (45) is a correspondent and the principal of a private English medium school. He has a post-graduate degree in English and in education as well. His educational qualifications tell him that he has to be considerate in giving homework keeping the age of the children in mind. But to withstand the competition from fellow correspondents/owners of schools he is compelled to increase the number of subjects. "What to do . I was rather forced to introduce Sanskrit and Hindi, classical music and dancing. I agree there is not enough place for our kids to play, once a week. Usually on Saturdays I will ask the teachers to allow the children to tell stories and display their talents in group singing and dancing. Apart from this, I cannot do anything but once I get enough money I wish to buy enough place to provide play ground and a good building for the children.

4

Manjula (30) is a teacher in a private English medium school. She is a science graduate with a degree in teaching. In her opinion, "English is not our mother-tongue. If we are to write fluently and freely we need to participate homework is one of the methods. The child will learn it better if he is made to write again and again. Every-day at least he has to spend three to four hours irrespective of his age."

"It is only during this age group children will have the ability to concentrate. If they learn to sit an hour or two and write again and again, it becomes a habit for them so that even in later life, they can easily attend to any hardwork and there will not be any need for the parents to ask their children to sit and read because by the time it becomes a part of their system and automatically the child sits and reads."

References

1. Bharathi, V.V. and Venkatalaxmi, K. (1992). "Medium of Instruction and Children's anxiety. *Indian Psychological Review*, No. 6-7.

2. Bharathi, V.V. and Venkatramaiah, S.R. (1976). Birth Order, Family size and Anxiety. *Child Psychiatry Quarterly,* 10(3) 11-19.

3. Buffie G.E. and Shane, G.H. (1977). Who does Johny's Homework *Parents and children.* Summer Vol. 15, p.29.

4. Chen Chuangheng and Stevenson H.W. (1989). Homework - A Cross Culture Examination. *Child Development* 60, 551 - 561.

5. Deepak Thimmaya (1993). All Play and no Work. *Sunday*, 11-17 April.

6. Deshpande and Saraswathi (1987). The Attitudes of Children and Parents Towards Homework.

7. Krishna Kumari, J. (1994). Academic Stress and Attitudes of Elementry School Children towards Homework. An unpublished Master's Thesis submitted to S.V. University, Tirupati (A.P.).

8. Kochar, S.K. (1985) *Methods and Techniques of teaching IInd Edition*, Prakasham Kendra, Lucknow. pp. 167-182.

9. Lalitha Sundaram (1992). Are home assignments necessary? *The Hindu*. February 4th, p. 18.

10. Lekha J. Shankar (1990). The burden of education. *Femina* No. 13 -27, p. 42.

11. Manjula, V. (1993). Attitudes of teachers towards homework - an unpublished Master's Degree Thesis submitted to S.V. University, Tirupati.

12. Mehar Dasthur (1989). Service of childhood years. *The illustrated Weekly*, 8th September, 1989.

13. Mittal (1991). Education is no child's play. *The Hindu,* July 31.

14. Newsitem (1992). *Andhrajyoti,* October 15th Daily, p.4.

15. Padmaja, K. (1991). Homework and Elementry School Children - Unpublished M.Sc. thesis submitted to S.V. University, Tirupati.

16. Paschal, A. (1985). The effects of Homework on learning - A Quantitative Analysis. *Journal of Education Research,* Vol. 78, pp. 97-104.

17. Prabha, S. (1989). Editorial of the Journal Third.

18. Prema, P. (1992). Letters to the editor. *The Hindu,* February 15.

19. Pruthesen Chowdary, Mirujain and Duiradutta (1994). No Admission Sunday, 19-26 April.

20. Raghuram Singh, M. (1994). To School Without tears, *The Hindu,* October 18.

21. S. Ramaswamy (1992). Homework - a Managerial perspective, *Journal of Experiments in Education*, vol. 20(7) 193-203.

22. Raja Gopalan (1995). The School Child's Burden. *The Hindu,* 14 October 1995.

23. Riti, M.D. (1995). Going home to school. *The week*, August 20.

24. Salnakureshy (1983). Homework and assignments. *Educational Review,* Vol. 80, p.80.

25. Saxena P.C. (1978). Adjustment of over and under achievers. *Indian Journal of Psychometry and Education,* (9) 25-33.

26. Sharma M.M. (1983). Homework in India and Abroad - *Educational Review,* Vol. 89, pp. 113 - 114.

27. Sinha L.S (1989). Homework - The Malady and the Cure. *The*

Hindu, September 5.

28. Special Correpondents 1993. To school without bag and Newsitem. To home without work. *The Hindu*, July 22.

29. Special correspondent 1995. The school bag load to continue. *The Hindu*, November 7.

30. Sudha Rani, G. (1993). Attitudes towards homework and intelligence of School Children - an unpublished M.Sc. Thesis to S.V. University.

31. Sudha Uma Shankar (1995). They are a Resilent lot. *The Hindu*, September, 5.

32. Suneetha, A. (1992). Influence of Mothers expectations on children's attitude towards homework - an unpublished M.Sc. Thesis submitted to S.V. University.

33. Venkata Subbaiah, M. (1994). Learning without burden *The Hindu*, May, 24th.

34. Venkateswara Rao, P. (1994). On your Marks. *Indian Express*, March 27.

Index